THE
IRISH
HERB
BASKET

*An Illustrated
Companion to Herbs*

Marigold heads and candles as a pretty table decoration

THE
IRISH
HERB
BASKET

*An Illustrated
Companion to Herbs*

TEXT BY HAZEL EVANS
PHOTOGRAPHY BY GLORIA NICHOL

GILL & MACMILLAN

THE IRISH HERB BASKET
An Illustrated Companion to Herbs

Written by Hazel Evans
Photography by Gloria Nicol

Designer: Jane Lanaway
Project editors: Veronica Sperling/Christine McFadden
Page makeup: Chris Lanaway
Step illustrations: Vana Haggerty
Border illustration: Pauline Allen

CLB 4882
© 1996 COLOUR LIBRARY BOOKS LTD

Published in Ireland by
Gill & Macmillan Ltd
Goldenbridge
Dublin 8
with associated companies throughout the world
ISBN 0 7171 2394 4

A catalogue record is available for this book from
the British Library

Origanum majorana · Mentha spicata · Calendula officinalis

CONTENTS

THE JOY OF HERBS

Sage

Sorrel

Savory

FRAGRANT, COLOURFUL herbs are not only among the most enchanting plants in any garden but also the most useful. They appeal to all our senses, even that of touch, with their wide range of shapes and textures.

Herbs have come down to us through history, but over the years we have lost much of the valuable knowledge of how to prepare, preserve and use them. Instead we have come to rely almost entirely on shops and markets for our food and drink, medicines and beauty preparations.

However, today, herbs are having a great revival as people realise what a vital part they have to play in our lives. There is nothing difficult about growing and using these helpful plants. If you can grow garden flowers then aromatics follow easily. If you can follow a recipe then you'll have no problems about making a fragrant potpourri, putting it out in bowls to perfume a room. Added to your food or steeped

in oils and vinegars, herbs bring sunshine indoors all winter long. And they offer so much more. They will scent your skin, enliven the colours of your clothes, make calming teas to sip on a summer evening and not only decorate your house but also keep insects at bay.

There is nothing more pleasant than to walk through your herb garden, however small it may be, at dusk on a summer's day, picking a leaf here and there, taking in the scents and perfumes, choosing what to use with a salad or a cooked dish. Even if you have no garden, you can still enjoy their company, for herbs will happily accommodate themselves on a window-sill, rewarding you not just with instant flavour for your food, but also the decorative effects of scent and colour. Discover exciting new ways that these unique plants can bring their subtle taste to your table and their distinctive fragrances to your home.

Marigold, one of the loveliest of garden herbs

PLANT CARE

BASIL
Ocimum basilicum

ABOVE *Basil can be grown easily from seed.*

Basil is a half-hardy annual. It grows up to 90 cm/36 in. high, though dwarf varieties reach only half that size. It needs a sunny site but should be protected from the wind and from direct overhead sunshine that might scorch its leaves, so place it near a hedge or a wall. It prefers a light, well-drained soil and hates heavy clay.

Basil cannot be put out into the garden until all danger of frost is past and it has to be sown afresh each year. The seeds are slow to germinate – the Greeks and Romans thought you should curse them as you sow them to make them sprout faster.

Start the plant off from seed by sowing it under cover in early spring in a temperature of 13°-15°C/55°-60°F, using small pots or latticed 'plug' trays. Avoid sowing it in open seed-boxes as the roots hate being disturbed.

Harden off the plants by moving them to a cooler place for a day or so, before placing outdoors. Alternatively you can sow them directly outdoors in late spring.

As the plant grows, pinch out the tops of flowering spikes to encourage them to bush out. Watch out for slugs and snails on young plants.

Water basil in the heat of the day; it should no longer be wet by the time the sun goes down.

Cut plants hard back in the autumn and bring them indoors to prolong their season.

12

BAY
Laurus nobilis

This evergreen tree is usually container-grown as then it can be protected against severe weather (-15°C/5°F or below) by being moved under cover. Bay likes plenty of sun, but prefers protection from the wind. It appreciates a rich, moist but well-drained soil.

Propagating bay is a long, slow process. Start it from seed by scattering the seed on the surface of barely moist soil in pots. Up-end a clear plastic sandwich bag over each pot and secure with an rubber band to act as a mini-hothouse. It needs to be kept at 18°C/65°F. Germination is slow and inclined to be unreliable. Remove the covering once the shoots are 2 cm/1 in. high.

Bay is raised professionally from cuttings in greenhouses where it can be misted constantly for a humid atmosphere. Raising it in pots under a plastic tent gives it the best chance of survival.

Grow bay from half-ripe cuttings taken in early autumn, covering the pot with a plastic bag. Keep warm until fresh shoots appear, then remove the bag. Plant out the following year.

BORAGE
Borago officinalis

Borage is a hardy annual, growing up to 90 cm/36 in. high. It likes a sunny, open position in the garden. It is a large, hairy, somewhat ungainly plant with grey-green leaves whose lax growth and untidy appearance is compensated for by its flowers. There is a white-flowered version too (*borago officinalis* 'Alba'), which is less often grown.

Grow borage in a light, well-drained soil that is not too rich. Choose a spacious patch because it will self-seed. Sow the seeds 5 cm/2 in. deep in the open where the plants are to grow in early spring. Thin the seedlings to 60 cm/24 in. apart.

Remove flowers as they fade to encourage a fresh crop and to avoid having too many seedlings. Dig up and discard plants that have finished flowering, as they will blacken and look unsightly after the first frosts.

The cut stems of borage are quite rough, so handle with care. Put them on the compost heap in the autumn as they contain nitrogen.

HARVESTING

NJOY YOUR herbs all year round. Harvest them when they are in their peak condition – usually in high summer – and dry them to use in the winter months, or to make them into preserves. Generally speaking, it is best to pick any herb before it flowers, when the aromatic oils are at their best.

Cut fresh green basil leaves for the kitchen as soon as they unfurl. They wilt very quickly, so harvest them just before you plan to use them.

Cut leaves for drying just before the plant flowers and on a dry day once the dew has gone. Handle them as little as possible, since bruising them in any way will cause them to lose the essential volatile oil that gives them their flavour.

It is worth trying to get one last crop of basil at the end of summer. In early autumn, cut the stems down to the base of the plant. Provided the weather is mild and there is some sun, you may get a crop of new shoots.

Allow some of your basil plants to flower so that you can collect seed for the following year. Once the seeds have fully formed, cut off the sprigs carefully and hang them to dry, fixing a paper bag over the tip of the stem, held in place with a small rubber band. That way the seeds will drop into it as they ripen. Sow in spring.

ABOVE *Keep pots of basil on a convenient shelf ready for snipping.*

14

LEFT *Cut borage should be immersed halfway up the stems in a jug of water.*

TIP
Mist your bay tree in hot, dry weather and shield the leaves from frost during winter if you want the tree to thrive.

Evergreen bay leaves can be harvested at any time of year. Take off individual leaves if possible, otherwise cut sprigs carefully so you do not damage the stem. Allow the leaves to dry before you use them as their flavour will then be stronger. If you have a large tree, sprigs of fresh bay make an ideal present if you are visiting someone. Town-dwellers, in particular, are always glad to have a bouquet of fresh herbs.

Harvest borage as it comes into flower, but only use the youngest leaves for salads as the old ones will be prickly and tough. Save larger leaves instead for sprigs to put in summer drinks. Take both leaves and flowers off the plant as you intend to use them, for the blooms in particular tend to wilt. Pick the flowers when they are just fully opened in late morning when they are free of dew.

MARINADES

THE PUNGENT FLAVOUR of bay makes it marvellous in marinades for meat dishes such as beef and pork, but it also goes unexpectedly well with fish. Bay also blends effectively with strong spices such as chilli and coriander, giving added zip to their flavours. Thread bay leaves between slices of onion, beef and tomato on kebab skewers to cook outdoors. Spear sea-fish such as red mullet with bay sprigs or simply lay the sprigs on a barbecue and arrange pork chops or beef steaks on top.

CLASSIC MARINADE FOR BEEF

❖ To each bay leaf add a sprig of herb – any of the classics, such as thyme or marjoram, go well with bay – plus 275 ml/8 fl oz dry red wine, 150 ml/4 fl oz water and 2 tbs olive oil.

BOUQUET GARNI

THE TRADITIONAL bouquet garni is made from 2 sprigs of parsley, 1 sprig of thyme and a bay leaf, but try these variations:

FOR BEEF PROVENÇAL
Bay with parsley, thyme, 2 cloves and 2 teaspoons of grated orange rind.

FOR LEMON PORK
Bay, parsley, thyme and a strip of lemon rind.

TO MAKE A BOUQUET GARNI

❖ To make your bouquet garni, wrap the herb sprigs in a piece of leek leaf to make a small package or tie together with string or wool. If you include small items like garlic or cloves, place the ingredients in a square of cheesecloth and tie with wool or string.

OILS AND VINEGARS

THE BEST herb vinegars are made with the aid of the sun: simply fill a bottle full of your chosen herb, pour vinegar over it and leave the bottle on a sunny window-sill or porch for two weeks, turning it from time to time. Then bring it indoors, filter it and re-bottle, adding a fresh sprig for decoration.

BAY VINEGAR

INGREDIENTS
Makes 550 ml/1 pt
bay leaves
550 ml/1 pt vinegar

Put the herb in a bowl then heat the vinegar to boiling point. Remove from the heat and pour it over the leaves.
Leave them to steep until the mixture cools, then strain and bottle with a fresh bay sprig inside.

BASIL OIL

INGREDIENTS
Makes 225 ml/8 fl oz
large handful basil leaves
225 ml/8 fl oz olive oil

Roughly chop the basil leaves. Crush in a mortar, gradually adding enough of the oil to turn them into a paste.
Spoon into a bottle and add the rest of the oil.

Stand the bottle on a sunny window-sill, turning and shaking it from time to time. Strain and check the flavour. If it is not strong enough, repeat the process using fresh basil. Finally, transfer the oil to a sterilized bottle and add a sprig of basil for decoration.

BASIL, BAY AND BORAGE

HERB OILS

Basil leaves can be perfectly preserved in oil to use in cooking later on. Fill a wide-necked bottle with freshly picked sprigs and cover them with sunflower oil to preserve them. Remove them individually as you want to use them. Save the oil to use in a special salad dressing.

19

AN ICE BOWL

A COLOURFUL HERB and flower ice bowl makes a marvellous centrepiece for a festive occasion and can be used to hold a variety of good things, from a summer punch to a sorbet or a fruit salad. You could also make small individual versions for chilled soups and, of course, ice cream.

❖ Buy an ice bowl mould or take 2 bowls of the same shape, one of them 1 inch smaller than the other (flexible plastic bowls are easiest to handle).

❖ Half fill the large basin with iced water then float the small one inside it, weighing it down until the two rims are level. Secure it in place with adhesive tape.

❖ Now push borage flowers, basil and bay leaves into the water between the basins, using a knitting needle to help distribute them evenly. Add ice cubes to stop the herbs rising to the top.

❖ Place the bowls in a freezer, making sure that they are absolutely level.

TIP
You could substitute baby vegetables for flowers in the ice bowl using it to serve crudités – slivers of carrot, celery, radish and root vegetables – served as an appetizer with a herb-flavoured dip.

❖ When you want to use your ice bowl, unmould it by wiping the inside of the small bowl with a wrung-out hot wet cloth or, if you are in a hurry, fill the small bowl with warm water. Twist and take out the small bowl, then place the large one briefly in warm water until it too can be twisted and detached. Place your ice bowl on a plate to catch any drips as it slowly starts to melt.

❖ If your ice bowl only makes a brief appearance, you can return it to the freezer to use over again.

TO MAKE THE BOWL

Weight the smaller bowl so it is level with the larger one and secure with tape.

BASIL, BAY AND BORAGE

IRISH
HERB
GARDENS

*Three herb
gardens in
Ireland worth
visiting are
to be found at
Ballymaloe
Cookery School,
Shanagarry, Co.
Cork, in the
kitchen garden
at Glin Castle,
Co. Limerick,
and at the
National
Botanic Gardens
at Glasnevin,
Dublin, where
the plot is based
on an eighteenth-
century design.*

LEFT *Herbs take to pots
without any problems.*

22

BASIL, BAY AND BORAGE

A VERY SMALL HERB GARDEN

Borage — Marjoram
Sage — Lemon balm
Mint — Mint
— Bay tree
Lemon-scented thyme — Chives
Common thyme — Common thyme
Basil — Basil

THIS VERY SMALL herb garden measures only 2 m/6 ft square but manages to encompass all the herbs you need to enliven your cooking. Its chosen focal point is a bay tree in a pot but it could equally well be a small fountain or a sundial.

Use flagstones between the beds for an old-fashioned look, but if you are uncertain of your skill in cutting them to form a circle, substitute gravel instead as it is much easier to lay.

If part of your garden is in shade, plant mint, chives, borage and lemon balm on that side. They need plenty of water but will produce lots of good greenery for cutting.

HERBS MAKE perfect companions for a patio. There are many decorative ways of growing basil and bay in pots, and even borage looks good when it takes centre stage in large tubs, surrounded by other herbs.

Paint your pots in bright colours – Mexican pinks and oranges, turquoise and white all look good against foliage. Use acrylic paints, they allow clay pots to breathe and won't wash off.

Buy the largest container you can find – it will not need watering so often. Always group small containers together for maximum effect and paint them in a matching or complementary colour scheme.

GROWING A STANDARD BAY

M OP-HEADED bay trees, grown as standards in pots, can cost a great deal of money but are easy to raise if you have a little patience. Start off from a rooted cutting.

❖ In autumn cut or carefully tear off a straight woody shoot about 20 cm/8 in. long with a heel on it (i.e. a piece of stem). Strip off the lower sets of leaves that might be covered with soil when the cutting is inserted, then push one-third of the cutting into a 80 cm/3 in. clay pot filled with a mixture of soil and sand and firm it down well. Carefully water it from the top and then firm it again. Set your cutting in a shady place indoors – in a shed, a garage or on a cool, shaded window-sill. Cover the whole pot with a large plastic bag, using a piece of twig to keep the 'tent' away from the leaves. In spring, check the cutting by giving it a light tug. If it has rooted, take it out into full light.

❖ Now transfer it into a 10 cm/4 in. pot filled with potting compost to which you should add half a teaspoonful of superphosphate or slow-release fertilizer. Push a 60 cm/24 in. bamboo stake down to the bottom of the pot alongside the stem, taking care not to touch the roots. Tie the bay cutting gently to it using raffia or knitting wool. Place the pot in a shaded place where it will have to reach for the light – this will make the stem grow longer faster. At this stage take off any side branches down the stem, one by one at weekly intervals, but leave any leaves as they help feed the plant.

❖ Once the 'trunk' of your cutting has reached the height you want it to be, pinch off the top growing tip. Now start taking off the lower leaves, keeping enough to bush out at the top.

❖ As the side shoots grow, pinch out their growing tips to give you a bushy ball shape. Move the plant to a larger pot each time the roots outgrow their container – a warning sign is if the plant has a top-heavy look or has roots coming through the bottom.

TIP

Be sure to feed your topiary tree
well, especially during its growing years.
If you are starting with a bought-in plant, choose
one that has a good straight stem, then
transfer it to a prepared pot and
continue as above.

BASIL, BAY AND BORAGE

1. *Place your cutting on a cool, shady window-sill. Cover completely with a plastic 'tent' supported with a twig to prevent it touching the leaves.*

2. *Re-pot in potting mixture with slow-release fertilizer. Stake and tie with twine or wool.*

3. *Pinch off the growing tip when the cutting has reached the required height. Remove the lower leaves to encourage the top to bush out.*

4. *Continue to pinch off the growing tips to achieve a ball-shaped topiary tree.*

LEFT *A full-grown topiary tree will last a lifetime.*

TIP
While your bay is being trained, be sure to feed it regularly.

PLANT CARE

N O HERB GARDEN should be complete without lavender and lovage. Apart from their many uses, they both have very attractive foliage – lavender's silvery needle-like leaves contrast beautifully with the glossy dark green stems of lovage. Coming from a tropical climate, lemongrass needs to be grown indoors and its bamboo-like shoots look good on a kitchen window-sill.

To grow lavender from cuttings, put several in one pot. To speed up rooting, put wire hoops over them and cover with a 'tent' made out of a clear plastic sandwich bag.

LAVENDER
Lavandula

A hardy evergreen shrub (but *stoechas* and *lanata* are tender varieties), lavender can grow up to 120 cm/48 in. but there are many compact varieties available. Lavender prefers sunshine and likes a light, well-drained soil that is not too rich. Put lavender plants 60 cm/24 in. apart. Sow lavender seeds on the surface of the soil in a seed tray in the autumn and give them some bottom heat if you can. Transfer the seedlings into pots containing well-drained compost; keep them in a cold greenhouse or cold frame until the spring. Let the roots get well established before you put them in the ground.

Lavender roots very easily. Take ripe cuttings in the autumn, setting several into a pot. Leave young plants indoors to overwinter.

Lavender should be cut back hard in the spring and trimmed after flowering.

LOVAGE
Levisticum officinale

This hardy perennial can grow up to 180 cm/ 72 in. in height. It can take partial shade and thrives in a moist fertile soil, but its roots should be protected in severe winters. Set your lovage plants 60 cm/24 in. apart. Keep them well watered for fresh supplies of foliage.

Sow seeds outdoors in the autumn and thin out in the spring. Take off the flowers as they appear to allow the roots to swell if you are using them for cookery. But allow some plants to flower in order to save the seeds.

Divide the clumps in the autumn and remove the large outside leaves.

SPLITTING A LOVAGE PLANT

When it has formed a large clump, lovage can be divided. Simply plunge two small hand forks, back to back, into the centre of the plant and pull them apart. If the clump is very large and the roots tough, you could chop it in half with a spade.

LEMONGRASS
Cymbopogon citratus

This perennial tropical grass grows like bamboo and achieves a height of up to 180 cm/72 in. in tropical conditions, but no more than 90 cm/36 in. in a container.

Lemongrass is normally grown from offsets planted in the spring.

The easiest way to raise your own is to buy some fresh lemongrass from an ethnic grocer or supermarket and put it in water, where it should sprout roots.

Lemongrass needs a temperature above 13°C/56°F at all times. It prefers a rich water-retentive soil (avoid lightweight composts) and needs constant moisture – mist it frequently and divide large clumps in autumn.

HOW TO PROPAGATE LEMONGRASS

You can raise your own plant with lemongrass bought from a shop, but make sure it is green and fresh-looking. Suspend a bundle in water until it sprouts whiskery roots, then separate and transfer to pots.

HARVESTING

GATHER THE FLOWERS of lavender early in the day, but after any dew has dried off them. Cut the stems at the base, even if you are planning to use only the tips; it will make the plant look tidier and the stems can be stored and used on open fires and in stoves.

ABOVE: *The delicate flowers of French lavender are easier to harvest if it is grown in a pot, like this specimen.*

A LAVENDER RACK

Pick the flowers just before they are fully open and tie the lavender spikes into bunches, ready for drying. It is easy to make a crisscross rack for lavender using twigs lashed together with raffia and suspended on hooks. If you are making lavender sheaves (see page 37), stand them upright to dry. Keep lavender flowers away from direct sunlight or they will fade.

LAVENDER, LOVAGE AND LEMONGRASS

LEFT: *Always harvest herbs like lemongrass, lovage and lavender freshly if you are planning to preserve them. Deal with them immediately.*

Cut lovage leaves fresh from the plant as you need them. Snip from the centre, as the outside leaves become coarse and tasteless in time. If you are planning to use the base of lovage stems and roots for cooking, earth up around the base of the plant to blanch it, which will take out the bitterness. Use a sharp knife to detach pieces for cooking. Replace the soil carefully afterwards.

Cut lemongrass as you want to use it for cooking. The fresh young green tips can be snipped off with scissors to chop and use in salads and other uncooked dishes. If it is grown in a decorative pot, bring the lemongrass straight to the table and let guests help themselves from the plant.

The lower part of the stem should be carefully cut or detached at soil level and used for longer cooked dishes – tie several together and put them to cook with meat in casseroles and curries, then remove before serving.

LAVENDER, LOVAGE AND LEMONGRASS

ORIENTAL SALAD

BOTH LOVAGE and lemongrass make flavourful additions to salads. Use the torn leaves of lovage instead of celery, which it resembles in taste. Don't be heavy-handed, however – get to know it first, for its leaves are very pungent. For a milder flavour, rub the leaves around a wooden salad bowl as you would a cut clove of garlic. Chop the tips of young shoots of lemongrass over exotic oriental salads like this one. Snip lemongrass over rice-based dishes for a subtle lemon flavour.

INGREDIENTS
Serves 4
125 g/4 oz mange-tout peas
125 g/4 oz baby sweetcorns
1 iceberg lettuce
½ red pepper
4 spring onions
2 young carrots
125 g/4 oz button mushrooms
2 tbs chopped lemongrass tips
4 lovage leaves
vinaigrette dressing
1 tsp honey

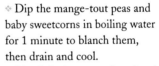

❖ Dip the mange-tout peas and baby sweetcorns in boiling water for 1 minute to blanch them, then drain and cool.

❖ Shred the lettuce and seed and slice the red pepper. Cut the onions, carrots and mushrooms into thin strips.

❖ Combine in a salad bowl with the peas, corn, lemongrass and torn lovage leaves.

❖ Top the salad with a vinaigrette dressing with a teaspoonful of honey beaten in.

TIP
If you like a spicy vinaigrette, add a teaspoonful of wholegrain mustard as well as honey to the mix.

LOVAGE AND CARROT QUICHE

LOVAGE GOES well with eggs, cheese and cream. It can be added to the classic Quiche Lorraine, but here is a different version. You can also add lovage to boiled or steamed carrots to bring out their flavour.

SHORTCRUST PASTRY

The classic recipe for shortcrust pastry is half fat to flour. A mix of margarine and lard gives the best texture. The type of flour you use will dictate how your shortcrust pastry behaves. Always add a pinch of salt. For a crunchier result, use half wholewheat flour, half white flour. In this case, use self-raising white flour as the wholewheat tends to make the pastry rather heavy.

TIP
When baking blind, brush the base of the quiche with beaten egg to seal it and keep the pastry crisp when the filling is added.

INGREDIENTS

Serves 4

225 g/8 oz shortcrust pastry
450 g/1 lb young carrots
50 g/2 oz butter
1 tbs chopped lovage leaves
50 g/2 oz grated Cheddar cheese
2 eggs, beaten
300 ml/ ½ pt single cream

❖ Roll out and bake the pastry blind in a flan tin.
❖ Clean the carrots and slice into thin discs. Fry them in the butter for 2 or 3 minutes, add a tablespoon water and simmer until they are just cooked but still firm – about 10 minutes.
❖ Remove from the heat, stir in the chopped lovage, grated cheese, beaten eggs and cream. Pour the mixture into the pastry case. Bake for 30 minutes in a preheated oven at 200°C/400°F/ gas mark 6. Serve piping hot, sprinkled with chopped fresh lovage.

LAVENDER, LOVAGE AND LEMONGRASS

Lavender looks good in a border.

LAVENDER, LOVAGE AND LEMONGRASS

PLANTING A LAVENDER HEDGE

HERBAL HEDGE not only makes an aromatic edge to a herb garden, but looks good around a flower border, too. The quickest and easiest way of creating a lavender hedge is to make one from container-grown cuttings which you have taken yourself or bought from a nursery.

TIP

Water your hedging plants well in the first few weeks. Remember, when they are fully grown they will need watering in periods of drought, as the thick bushy growth will stop moisture reaching the roots.

1. Use a length of twine and two pegs to mark a straight line, or a length of hose to make a curve, and make a row of holes where your plants are to go. Sprinkle a little organic fertilizer in and around the site.

2. Working as quickly as possible so that the roots are not exposed to the elements, set your plants into the ground. Full-size lavenders should be set 60 cm/24 in. apart, smaller varieties like Munstead 30 cm/12 in. apart.

3. Clip the tops regularly to encourage side growth. Once the hedge is established, cut it back severely each spring, and, as it grows, trim it so that the sides slope a little and the base is broader than the top.

A DRIED LAVENDER SHEAF

SHEAVES OF DRIED lavender look very chic but cost a great deal. Here's how to make one for yourself at a fraction of the price. Harvest the lavender when it is at its best – when the flowers are just about to come out.

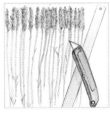

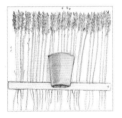

1. Lay the lavender spikes on a board, matching up their tips so that they are exactly in line with each other.

2. Measure the length of the stalks by placing your chosen container a suitable distance from the tips. Then trim the base of the stalks. Secure with a rubber band. Stand somewhere warm and well ventilated to dry, out of direct light.

3. When the lavender is completely dry, wrap the middle of the spikes with a piece of florist's wire, taking care it does not cut into the stems. Push the stems into a pot containing moss.

TIP
If you leave
the harvested
lavender spikes to
dry and harden for a
day or two before
using, they are
easier to
handle.

37

PLANT CARE

Clip pot-grown mints and marjorams frequently to keep them bushy.

MARJORAM
Origanum

This herb grows to a height of up to 30 cm/12 in. depending on the variety. It needs a sunny situation and a well-drained soil, preferring one that is alkaline (chalky). It tends to become woody at the base with leggy shoots, so it should be trimmed back from time to time and some of the dead wood cut away. Divide over-large clumps, since if marjoram becomes tough and overgrown its flavour deteriorates. Pull off some pieces of root in autumn, pot them and bring them indoors to grow under cover and give you winter greenery.

MINT
Mentha

Mint is a perennial plant which grows up to 60 cm/24 in. high from creeping roots that spread very rapidly and, if you are not careful, can soon take over a corner of the garden. Mint will grow almost anywhere in the garden and enjoys the shade. If you are short of space, it is best to plant it in a bottomless bucket sunk in the ground. Mint is best grown from pieces of root or cuttings, as it does not always come true to form if you start it from seed. Snip the plants frequently and pinch out the flowers to keep the plants bushy and encourage plenty of young growth, which is what you need. Bring one or two roots indoors and grow the plant in pots to give you supplies of fresh mint in midwinter.

1. To keep mint from encroaching on the plants around it, take the bottom out of a tin or bucket, sink it in the ground, then plant the mint in the centre.

MARIGOLD
Calendula officinalis

Marigold is a hardy annual, grown each year from seed and reaching a height of up to 60 cm/24 in. It prefers the sun and will grow in almost any soil as long as it is not waterlogged. Sow marigold in the spring in a sunny place and thin the seedlings out to 25 cm/10 in. apart. Or start it off in pots in autumn, or sow it, one seed at a time, in divided seedtrays, transferring the seedlings to pots later on. Once fully established, marigold will go on to seed itself from year to year.

1. To sow marigolds, put several seeds in a pot, and cover them with potting mixture. Keep the soil moist at all times.

2. When the seedlings are large enough to handle, transfer them carefully into individual pots.

Marigold petals make a vivid display.

HARVESTING

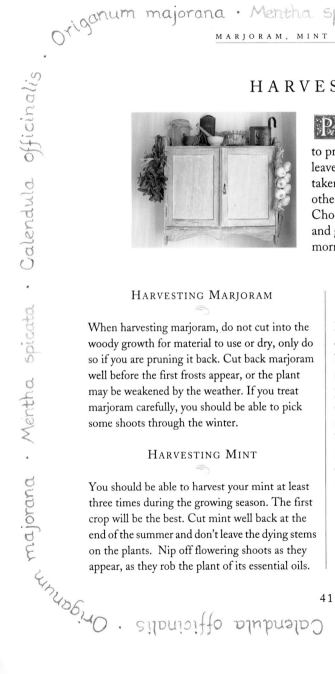

PICK YOUR herbs early in the growing season to encourage them to produce vigorous new growth. The leaves of mint and marjoram should be taken before the plant starts to flower, otherwise the flavour will be less strong. Choose only the best parts of the plant and gather them on a dry day, after the morning dew has dried.

HARVESTING MARJORAM

When harvesting marjoram, do not cut into the woody growth for material to use or dry, only do so if you are pruning it back. Cut back marjoram well before the first frosts appear, or the plant may be weakened by the weather. If you treat marjoram carefully, you should be able to pick some shoots through the winter.

HARVESTING MINT

You should be able to harvest your mint at least three times during the growing season. The first crop will be the best. Cut mint well back at the end of the summer and don't leave the dying stems on the plants. Nip off flowering shoots as they appear, as they rob the plant of its essential oils.

HARVESTING MARIGOLDS

Pick the flowers of marigold just as they fully open. Leave the blooms for about half an hour before taking the petals off, then they will come away from the centre more easily. If you are picking whole marigold flowers for drying, cut off the stem as well, don't leave a stump. If you are collecting marigold seed, make sure that it is brown and fully ripe before you raid the plants. Removing the seed heads will encourage more blooms.

41

RICH BEEF CASEROLE WITH MARIGOLD

COPY THE medieval housewife and put some marigold petals in your casseroles. They will help to give a rich brown colour and add a delicate yet distinctive flavour.

INGREDIENTS
Serves 4
700 g/1½ lb stewing steak
1 large onion
2 green peppers
2 tbs oil
150 ml/¼ pt red wine
2 tbs tomato purée
2 tbs freshly picked marigold petals

❖ Cut the meat into small cubes. Peel and slice the onion, seed and slice the peppers. Heat the oil in a frying pan and sauté the onion until golden brown. Remove with a slotted spoon and place in a casserole. Fry the peppers until they have wilted, then add them to the onion. Brown the meat on all sides. Pour on the wine, stir in the tomato purée and bring to the boil. Add to the casserole, add the marigold petals and stir.
❖ Cover and cook in a preheated oven at 170°C/325°F/gas mark 3 for about 2½ hours.

PORK PROVENÇAL WITH MARJORAM

THE COMBINATION of slivers of orange peel and the marjoram gives this slow-cooked dish a delicious flavour.

INGREDIENTS
Serves 4
2 onions
1 green pepper
1 red pepper
125 g/4 oz mushrooms
2 tbs flour
700 g/1½ lb sliced pork fillet
50 ml/2 fl oz olive oil
350g/12 oz can tomatoes
2 strips orange peel
1 tbs chopped marjoram

❖ Peel and slice the onions, seed and slice the peppers and slice the mushrooms. Season the flour and coat the slices of pork in it. Fry the onions in the oil, then add the pork and fry until browned. Remove with a slotted spoon and put into a casserole. Fry the peppers and mushrooms until tender, then add the tomatoes. Transfer to the casserole, add the orange peel and marjoram.
❖ Cover and cook in a preheated oven at 180°C/350°F/gas mark 4 for 1½ hours.

43

HERB SALADS

USE MARJORAM, mint and marigold for tasty salads,
homing in on Mediterranean leaves like radicchio
and the peppery rocket. Chop the marjoram and mint,
and scatter marigold petals on top for extra colour.

44

MINT AND CUCUMBER SALAD

M INT AND CUCUMBER make a perfect partnership. Try this cooling side salad or appetiser, substituting yogurt for the vinaigrette if you wish.

INGREDIENTS

Serves 4
1 cucumber
150 ml/ ¼ pt vinaigrette
2 tbs chopped mint

❖ Peel the cucumber and slice it very thinly. Sprinkle the slices with salt and put them in a colander set over a plate.
❖ Put a weight on top and leave the cucumber to drain for 30 minutes.
❖ Transfer to a serving dish and pour on the vinaigrette, then top with the chopped mint.
❖ Leave to marinate for a further 30 minutes before serving.

TIP
If your cucumber slices look limp, put them in iced water for a while to revive them.

TOMATO AND MARJORAM SALAD

Y OU CAN substitute the more pungent oregano for marjoram in this salad. If you use the herb in dried form, halve the quantity.

INGREDIENTS

Serves 4
1 clove garlic
150 ml/ ¼ pt vinaigrette
4 large tomatoes
3tbs finely grated Parmesan cheese
1 tbs chopped marjoram

❖ Make several slits in the garlic clove and put it in the vinaigrette.
❖ Leave for at least 1 hour, and preferably overnight.
❖ Slice the tomatoes and put them in a shallow dish. Season well with salt and pepper and sprinkle with the Parmesan.
❖ Remove the garlic clove from the vinaigrette and pour the dressing over the tomatoes.
❖ Top with the chopped marjoram and serve with warm, crusty bread.

MINT TEA

The best mint to use is Moroccan mint (*Mentha viridis*). Failing that, use peppermint. Sometimes in winter the Moroccans add sweet marjoram to the mint.

INGREDIENTS

Makes 900 ml/1 1/2 pt

1 1/2 tbs green tea (available from specialist tea suppliers)
handful of whole mint leaves
150-175g/5-6 oz lump sugar

❖ Rinse out a teapot with boiling water. Put in the tea and cover with the mint. Add the sugar and fill the teapot with boiling water.

❖ Leave to draw for 5 minutes, taking care that the mint does not rise above the surface of the water.

❖ Pour out into small glasses.

❖ In Morocco they make two pots of tea at a time and pour the liquid from both pots at the same time into the glasses.

MINT LIQUEUR

SERVE THIS unusual liqueur well chilled in small glasses as an after-dinner drink, or try it as an apéritif with tasty morsels of smoked fish. Toss it back, Russian style, in one shot.

INGREDIENTS

Makes 1 litre/1³⁄₄ pt

225 ml/8 fl oz tightly packed peppermint leaves

1 litre/1³⁄₄ pt vodka

100 g/4 oz sugar

MINT JULEP

INGREDIENTS

Makes 850 ml/1¹⁄₄ pt

150 ml/¹⁄₄ pt water

4 tbs chopped mint

2 tbs sugar

juice of 1 lemon

425 ml/4 fl oz sparkling mineral water

120 ml/4 fl oz whiskey

❖ Boil the water and pour it over the mint. Add the sugar and stir until dissolved. Add the lemon juice, then leave the mixture to cool.

❖ Strain into a jug, stir in the mineral water and the whiskey. Pour onto ice cubes in tall glasses, add a sprig of mint and serve.

❖ Put the mint in a wide-necked jar and cover with the vodka.

❖ Put on the lid, shake well, then leave to steep for 2 weeks.

❖ Add the sugar and steep for 2 more weeks, shaking the jar from time to time to dissolve the sugar.

❖ Strain the liqueur into a fresh bottle, add a sprig of mint for decoration.

❖ Leave for a further 2 weeks before drinking.

MARJORAM, MINT AND MARIGOLD

PAINTED HERB POTS

MARIGOLDS make stunning decorative motifs with their bright and colourful blooms. With a little practice, you can paint the flowers freehand to decorate terracotta plant pots, or embellish an old enamel breadbox or a set of storage canisters for the kitchen. When painting in such a free way, spontaneity is more important than precision, so try painting some flowers first on waste paper until you get the hang of it and build up your confidence.

MATERIALS

*piece of natural sponge
acrylic paints in bright
blue and an assortment of
yellow, orange, red and
brown shades
flat brush*

TIP

Don't restrict your artistry to flowers – suns, moons and rainbows are equally attractive. Collect inspiring images from magazines and books.

1. Using an old plate or a piece of waste paper as a palette, squeeze out some blue paint and add a little water to it. Dab the sponge into the paint and lightly press the sponge all over the pot to leave a mottled pattern. Leave to dry completely.

2. Squeeze blobs of yellow, orange and red paint closely together on your palette. Mix them together slightly with the brush, so that the mixture is streaky and the overall colour is a deep orange. Paint naive flower shapes onto the pot, with strips of streaky colour radiating out from the centre.

Leave to dry. Repeat the process again, painting a smaller flower in lighter tones within those already worked. Leave to dry.

3. To make the flower centres, dab the middles of the flowers a few times with the brush loaded with a deeper colour. Leave to dry.

KITCHEN SACHETS

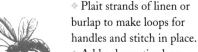

AKE THE MOST of marjoram's insect-repellent properties by growing plenty to make into kitchen sachets or herb bags for the wardrobe and linen closet. A few dried marigold petals add colour and fragrance. In the Middle Ages, it was said that a bag containing a wolf's tooth and marigold petals wrapped in bay leaves, kept under the pillow at night, would enable you to see what burglars were up to in the dark.

MATERIALS

rectangles of coarse linen or burlap 15 × 20 cm/8 × 6 in.
handful of dried marjoram
small marigolds

* Make up small bags with the linen or burlap, gluing the side and bottom.
* Fill with dried herbs and glue the top.

* Plait strands of linen or burlap to make loops for handles and stitch in place.
* Add a decorative bow.

TIP
If you use a really open-weave fabric like cheesecloth, you can add fresh marigolds to your herb-filled sachets and let them dry inside. Otherwise dry your marigolds in the usual way and crumble the petals.

MARJORAM, MINT AND MARIGOLD

51

PLANT CARE

ROSEMARY
Rosmarinus officinalis

Rosemary is an evergreen perennial shrub which grows up to 90 cm/36 in. high and prefers a sunny, sheltered spot. It needs a well-drained soil and, once full-grown, dislikes being moved.

Rosemary is very much an all-purpose plant. You can start it from seed undercover, in a seed-tray or in pots, but it prefers some bottom heat. Take cuttings from non-flowering shoots in mid or late summer. If your winters are harsh, overwinter the plant in a cold frame. You can also root sprigs in spring by suspending them in a glass of water. Rosemary can also be layered. Simply peg down a low-growing branch, making a small cut in the underside of the stem, and cover it with soil. Anchor it with a hoop made from a small piece of wire or a large hairpin.

1. Set rosemary cuttings out in a tray of soil in late summer. In harsh winters, keep in a cold frame or cold greenhouse. Cuttings should have rooted by the spring.

RUE
Ruta graveolens

This hardy perennial grows to a height of 60 cm/24 in. and likes a sunny spot. It does best in thin or poor soil.

Rue can be grown from seed which should be mixed with a little sand when sowing as the seeds are so fine. The hybrid 'Jackman's Blue', however, should be started from softwood cuttings taken in early summer.

Cut mature plants back in the spring to stop them from becoming spindly and again in mid-summer after flowering. Divide large plants when necessary. Protect variegated rue from hard frosts in winter.

THE ROSE
Rosa

Plant roses any time from autumn to early spring. Roses are 'greedy feeders' so dig in plenty of manure around them. If your rose is bare-rooted, make a little mound beneath the base of the plant, then spread out the roots like the spokes of an umbrella. If your rose has been grafted onto a rootstock (look for the scar on the stem) make sure the graft is just above soil level.

Shake the plant gently from time to time as you fill in the soil around it. Tread the topsoil firmly with your feet to anchor the rose in place.

1. Plant roses on a dry day when there is no cold, prevailing wind. If the day is too cold, store the plant in a bucket of water under cover for later planting. Dig a hole wide enough to take the plant comfortably.

2. Make a little mound of soil in the hole, where the base of the plant is to go. Then put the plant in place, spreading its roots out as you go.

3. Scatter a little bone-meal around the roots, then fill with soil. Check that the scar on the stem is above ground level if the rose is grafted.

4. Shake the plant from time to time as you fill in the soil to make sure no air pockets are left around the roots. Tamp down the soil around the bush.

HARVESTING

FRAGRANT rosemary, rue and rose have many uses from potpourri to desserts. Use them fresh if you can, but dry some to use during the winter months.

HARVESTING ROSEMARY

You can harvest rosemary all year round. Flowering shoots should be picked in the middle of the day after the dew has disappeared from the blooms. Pick the top fourth only of full-grown plants for the best results in cooking or drying. The best quality of all is cut from the plant before it has flowered.

TIP
To retain maximum potency, store your dried herbs in sealed jars kept in a dark place, rather than a paper bag.

HARVESTING RUE

If you want to dry rue, cut back the top half of the plant in spring and again after it has flowered. The flowering sprigs can also be cut to use in flower decoration or to dry. Wear rubber gloves, or wash your hands immediately after handling rue, as the sap can blister the skin.

HARVESTING ROSES

Always use pruning-shears when harvesting roses. Pick buds for drying when they are still tight-packed, or just before they open if you are using them as cut flowers.

If you are picking rose petals for food, make sure that you take them from plants that have not been sprayed with herbicide or insecticide. Petals for potpourri should be harvested just as the flowers are beginning to look blousy and overblown.

If the stems are hard and woody, hammer the ends gently or make a short vertical cut up the base of each stem and discard any foliage that will end up under water. Then put the roses in a bowl of tepid water and make a slanting cut across the bottom tips of the stems again, under water. This eliminates any air bubbles that may have formed in the stems when they were first cut.

Leave rosehips on the bushes as long as possible before picking them, so that they have time to mature.

<u>ROSEMARY, RUE AND ROSE</u>

ABOVE *A bowl of fallen petals makes an
attractive display for the table.*

ROSEMARY, RUE AND ROSE

ROAST LAMB AND ROSEMARY

LAMB AND rosemary make a perfect partnership, for the herb not only perfumes the meat but counteracts its tendency toward greasiness.

MAKE NEAT pockets in a leg or shoulder of lamb and tuck sprigs of rosemary inside. Or cut slits in the skin and poke single leaves in place, or strew the leaves on top. Baste the joint well with the dripping as it cooks, then use the fat as a basis of a rich, rosemary-flavoured gravy.

Use rosemary, too, on the barbecue: burn little bundles of it among the charcoal, or lay lamb chops to grill on sprigs over a fire. Wrap whole baby poussins with rosemary and other herbs in kitchen foil and put to slow-cook on a barbecue grid.

CARAMEL ONIONS WITH ROSEMARY

INGREDIENTS

Serves 4

4 large onions
25 g/1 oz softened butter
1 tbs brown sugar
1 tbs rosemary leaves

TIP

Make your own caramelized onion preserve or 'jam' to serve with meats. Cook onion slices with brown sugar, a little butter, a dash of sherry, and a little dried rosemary. Bottle and store.

❖ Peel the onions and cut a sliver off the top of each so you have a flat surface. Cook the onions whole, in boiling salted water, for about 20 minutes, then remove and drain.

❖ Mix the butter with the sugar. Arrange the onions close together in an ovenproof dish and spread the flat tops with the butter/sugar mix. Sprinkle with the rosemary leaves.

❖ Bake in a preheated oven at 200°C/400°F/gas mark 6 for about 30 minutes, until the onions are cooked and golden brown.

❖ Alternatively, arrange the onions around a roast in the roasting-pan.

ROSE PETAL SORBET

THE DELICATE perfume of the rose is delicious in desserts. Try adding it to your favourite recipe for home-made ice cream, or use it in a sweet soufflé. Never take petals from bushes that have been sprayed with chemicals.

INGREDIENTS

Serves 4

125 g/4 oz caster sugar

425 ml/³/₄ pt water

grated rind and juice of 2 lemons

340 g/12 oz scented rose petals

2 tsp rosewater

1 egg white

❖ Put the sugar, water and grated lemon rind in a saucepan. Boil briskly, stirring until the sugar has completely dissolved, then simmer for 6 minutes.

❖ Remove from the heat, add the rose petals, and cool. Strain into a bowl and add the lemon juice and rosewater. Pour into a shallow icetray to freeze for 2 hours or until mushy.

❖ Decant the mixture into a bowl. Stiffly whisk the egg white and fold it in.

❖ Return the mixture to the freezer and re-freeze completely. Serve in scoops in sundae glasses.

ROSE PETAL SYLLABUB

INGREDIENTS

Serves 4

a handful of scented rose petals

150 ml/¹/₄ pt medium sweet white wine

300 ml/¹/₂ pt double cream

juice of ¹/₂ lemon

2 egg whites

200 g/4 oz rose-scented caster sugar

❖ Infuse the rose petals overnight in the wine, then drain off the wine and reserve. Whip the cream and mix with the wine and lemon juice in a bowl. Whisk the egg whites until they are stiff, fold in the sugar, then fold the egg whites into the wine mix.

❖ Pour the mixture into sundae glasses and chill well. Serve decorated with rose petals.

ROSEMARY, RUE AND ROSE

A DRIED ROSEMARY TREE

LITTLE TREES made from dried rosemary make pretty decorations for a shelf, a side-table or on a dining-room table. They can be made from fresh rosemary which is left to dry *in situ*, but dried rosemary twigs are easier to handle and poke into place more firmly. Your tree could be in any one of a number of topiary silhouettes – ball-shaped, conical or even square.

MATERIALS

terracotta pot
piece of plastic sheeting
plaster of Paris
piece of branch for the tree 'trunk'
glue
oasis ball, cone or square
Sphagnum moss
twine or florist's wire
handful of dried rosemary sprigs
about 13 cm/5 in. long

1. Line the pot with a piece of plastic. Mix up the plaster of Paris to a thick paste with water and pour it into the pot.

2. Before the plaster has set, stick the 'trunk' into the pot. When it is firm and the plaster has dried, spread some glue on the top of the trunk and push the oasis onto it.

3. Cover the oasis with Sphagnum moss, fixing it in place with twine or florist's wire. Push the rosemary sprigs into the moss until the top is completely covered.

HUNGARY WATER

HERBS HAVE BEEN used throughout the ages to make fragrant toilet waters to freshen and scent the body. Flowering tops of rosemary and roses macerated in alcohol are the the basic ingredients of Hungary Water, one of the most ancient perfumes. It was invented in 1370 by a hermit for the 72-year-old Dionna Izabella, the Queen of Hungary, to make 'a young face exceedingly beautiful, an old face very tolerable'. She claimed that it so improved her health and strength that 'on beholding my beauty the King of Poland desired to marry me…'

INGREDIENTS

Makes 900 ml/1¹/₂ pt

40 g/2 oz rosemary, preferably flowering tops
25 g/1 oz scented rose petals
25 g/1 oz mint
2 tbs grated lemon rind
300 ml/¹/₂ pt rosewater
300 ml/¹/₂ pt orangeflower water
300 ml/¹/₂ pt vodka

1. Pound the rosemary leaves with the rose petals and mint. Add the grated lemon rind. Transfer to a wide-mouthed jar and cover with the rosewater, orangeflower water and vodka.

2. Leave to steep for 2 weeks, then strain into a bottle and seal tightly. Leave to mature for a month before using.

EAU DE COLOGNE

EAU DE COLOGNE was invented in the eighteenth century. If you have difficulty in finding bergamot leaves you could use 10 drops of the essential oil instead.

INGREDIENTS

Makes 300 ml/¹/₂ pt

25 g/1 oz bergamot leaves
50 g/2 oz rosemary leaves
grated rind of 1 orange
grated rind of 1 lemon
3 drops neroli oil
300 ml/¹/₂ pt vodka

❖ Put all the ingredients in a wide-mouthed jar and cover with the vodka. Leave to macerate for 3 weeks, shaking the jar from time to time.
❖ Strain off into a clean bottle and leave for at least 2 weeks to mature.

63

ROSEMARY, RUE AND ROSE

RICH ROSE POTPOURRI

I N THIS potpourri, the scents of the different layers of dried herbs combine with time to give a delicious fragrance. Keep the potpourri for at least six weeks before use. Keeping it well sealed will improve the scent.

INGREDIENTS

550 ml/1 pt dried pink and red rose petals
550 ml/1 pt dried mint leaves
50 g/2 oz dried rue sprigs
550 ml/1 pt dried red rosebuds
50 g/2 oz dried rosemary flowers and leaves
1/4 vanilla bean
25 g/1 oz orris root
2 tsp ground cinnamon
1/2 tsp ground cloves
5 drops rose oil
5 drops rosemary oil
1 drop patchouli oil

They are not long,
the days of wine and roses
Out of a misty dream
Our path emerges for a while, then closes
Within a dream.
ERNEST DOWSON

1. *Put the dried herbs into separate bowls. Chop the vanilla pod finely, mix together with the orris root, cinnamon and cloves. Mix the oils together in a cup.*

2. *Put the dried herbs in a wide-mouthed jar in layers, starting with rose petals, then a layer of mint and rue, then rosebuds and finally the rosemary. On each layer sprinkle over a little of the orris, cinnamon and clove mixture and a drop or two of the oil mixture. Finish with a layer of rose petals.*

PLANT CARE

SAGE
Salvia officinalis

AGE IS A perennial plant and an evergreen and will grow to a height of around 60 cm/24 in. It likes a fertile soil if it can get it and some sun, but otherwise will survive in almost any garden surroundings, as long as the ground is well drained. Provided you cut it back to base in the spring, it will turn in time into a small, good-looking bush that will flourish for many years.

Sow common and clary sage in the spring where they are to grow. Take cuttings from the variegated varieties as they do not always grow true to form from seed. Plant out the cuttings in the autumn. Old sage plants which have become 'leggy' can be layered very successfully by pegging a branch down and covering it with soil. Plants need to be replaced every 4-7 years.

1. Take cuttings from mid-summer to the end of summer. Using a clean, sharp knife, cut off a non-flowering sideshoot 10–15 cm/4–6 in. long. Cut off the stem just below a set of leaves.

2. Dip the end of the cutting in water then in rooting powder, shake off the excess and plant the cutting firmly in a pot of suitable compost.

SORREL
Rumex acetosa, Rumex scutatus

 ORREL, *R. acetosa*, is a lush green perennial which usually grows up to 45 cm/18 in. high but can reach 60 cm/24 in. in a wet summer. Sorrel will grow almost anywhere but prefers a moist acid soil and some shade.

Sow the seed in spring and thin the seedlings out to 22 cm/9 in. apart as they grow. A little sorrel goes a long way – a dozen plants will be more than enough. As the flowers arrive, cut the stems to the ground and fresh shoots will appear. Divide the plants regularly in spring or autumn, as if they become too tightly packed they will attract the attention of snails. French or buckler leaf sorrel, *R. scutatus,* grows to a height of 30-45 cm/12-18 in. Unlike *R. acetosa*, it prefers a dry soil. Sow the seed in shallow drills, then thin the seedlings first to 7 cm/3 in. then to 15 cm/6 in. apart as they grow. Pinch out the tiny green flowers to encourage new growth.

1. To thin the seedlings, lift and replant 22 cm/9 in. apart, taking care not to damage the delicate roots. Alternatively, simply uproot unwanted seedlings for use in salads.

SAVORY
Satureia montana, Satureia hortensis

INTER SAVORY, *S. montana*, is a shrubby perennial that keeps its leaves most of the year round. It grows to a height of about 30 cm/12 in. tall and likes to be in full sun in a well-drained soil.

Sow the seed where it is to grow in early autumn or in the spring. Thin the seedlings to 15-22 cm/6-9 in. apart when they are large enough to handle. Alternatively, divide the roots in early spring or take cuttings in early summer. Winter savory needs to be replaced every 2-3 years as it becomes very woody.

Summer savory, *S. hortensis*, is a half-hardy annual which grows from 20-30 cm/8-12 in. high. Like winter savory, it prefers the sun and it must have a well-drained soil. Sow summer savory in the spring where it is to grow. For a winter supply, sow in the early autumn to grow in pots in the greenhouse. Although summer savory is an annual, once you have raised a patch from seed it will self-sow from then onward, giving you a fresh crop of plants each spring.

TIP
Take cuttings of winter savory in the autumn, pot them up and bring them indoors for fresh young growth in winter.

HARVESTING

T HE BEST TIME for collecting herbs is late morning on a sunny, warm day after the dew has dried. Never pick plants that are wet and always check them for insects. Any plant that is going to be used for cooking must be one that has not been sprayed with herbicide or insecticide.

Don't stuff your herbs into a bag, you will crush them and release some of their valuable essential oils. Lay them out gently in a wide, flat basket.

Don't pick more than you can deal with at one time.

Pick leaves when the flowers on the plant are still in bud, don't strip too many off the stem or you may damage it. Pick flowers just before they open.

HARVESTING SAGE

The best time to cut the fresh stems is in early summer – sage leaves can turn leathery later on. Plants that have flowered will have lost some of their pungent power. Inspect the leaves for any insects or signs of disease. Once sage has become twiggy, you can pick some sprigs and keep them on hand in the kitchen, helping yourself to leaves when you need them.

LEFT *The freshly harvested leaves of sage can be added sparingly to tomato dishes and stews.*

TIP
After you have cut down your sorrel plants, watch for the first fresh green tips and snip them off to use in salads.

68

HARVESTING SORREL

Pick only the fresh, young, succulent leaves of sorrel as you want to use them, or freeze them right away. Sorrel is at its best in early summer, later on the leaves tend to become bitter. Inspect the leaves for baby snails which love to lurk on their undersides, and rinse them thoroughly before using. Tear off the stems, which can be stringy and tough, and use only the leaves in cookery. The leaves cook very quickly, turning to a purée almost immediately.

HARVESTING SAVORY

Harvest savory in the early morning before the heat of the midday sun leaches out the natural oils. Then hang bunches of sprigs in the shade for the dew to dry off them before packing them away. Pick savory leaves when they are relatively young. The older stems, which can become leathery towards the end of summer, are best used for decoration – on top of small cheeses for instance.

LEFT *Always deal with sorrel leaves the moment you harvest them.*

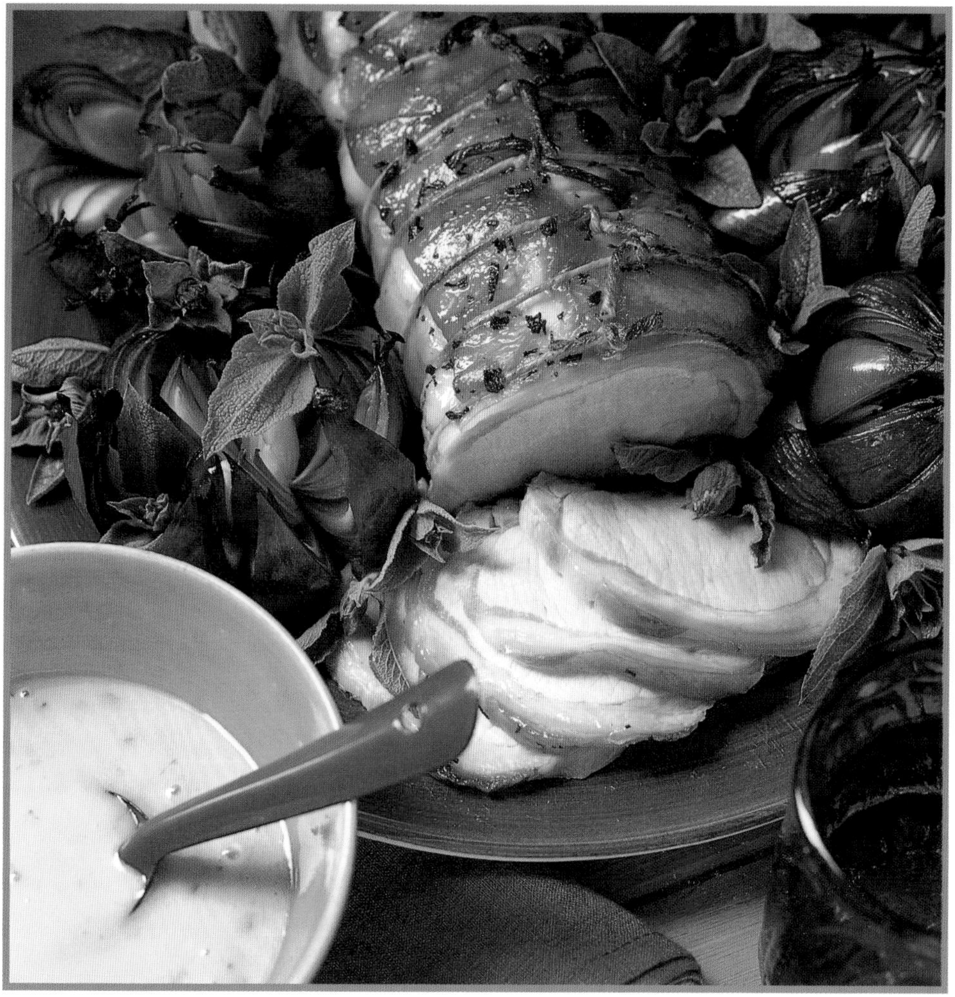

REAL SAGE-AND-ONION STUFFING

AGE IS THE basic ingredient in most packet stuffings, but try making your own with fresh leaves and you'll be delighted with the difference. Savory can be used in a stuffing or dressing too, for a different flavour.

INGREDIENTS

Serves 4

1 onion
a knob of butter
fresh breadcrumbs
3 tbs chopped fresh sage or 2 tsp dried sage
1 large egg
4 tbs milk

* Peel and chop the onion.
* Melt the butter in a frying pan and gently fry the onion for about 7 minutes or until slightly coloured.
* Remove the pan from the heat and stir in the breadcrumbs. Add salt and pepper to taste and stir in the chopped sage.
* Beat the egg lightly.
* Add the milk and stir into the mix.
* Use to stuff a pork roast or cook and serve as an accompaniment.

TIP

Always save leftover scraps of bread. Grind them in a food processor to reduce them to crumbs, then freeze them in plastic bags to use in stuffings.

HERB BUTTERS

ERB BUTTERS are very easy to make and will store for a long time in the refrigerator, indefinitely in the freezer. Make a selection to keep on hand. Chill the butter, cut and wrap in small segments, or save in small pots so that you can defrost it quickly and easily to liven up a meal. A pot of chilled herb butter is delicious on grilled steak or chicken, and on fish too. The flavour is released as the butter melts and mingles with the cooking juices.

SAVORY BUTTER

Spread this butter on bread to go with cheeses of all kinds. Savory goes well with garlic, so add some to the mix if the idea appeals to you.

INGREDIENTS
Makes 125 g/4 oz
125 g/4 oz butter
2 tbs finely chopped savory

❖ Melt the butter slowly in a saucepan, add the chopped savory and cook for two minutes, stirring constantly. Take the pan off the heat, and leave to stand for 30 minutes.
❖ Reheat and strain off the herb. Pour the butter into little ceramic pots and decorate with fresh sprigs of savory.

SAGE BUTTER

It is best to use dried rather than fresh sage for this butter, otherwise the texture of fresh leaves makes it difficult to spread.

INGREDIENTS
Makes 125 g/4 oz
125 fl/4 oz butter
1 tsp lemon juice
2 tsp dried sage

❖ Soften the butter with a fork and work in the lemon juice drop by drop, then the dried sage. Put the mix in the refrigerator to chill until firm.
❖ Turn out onto greaseproof paper and shape into a square before serving. Or cut into strips, wrap each one separately and freeze.

HERBAL PLACE MATS

A POTPOURRI of dried herbs gives out a delicious aroma under a hot pan, plate or teapot if you encase the herbs in decorative mats. The mats are made from mattress ticking but you could use any other fabric you choose.

POTPOURRI

Makes 1

dried rind of 1 lemon
300 ml/ ½ pt dried rosemary
300 ml/ ½ pt dried thyme
550 ml/1 pt dried sage
300 ml/ ½ pt dried savory
2 cinnamon sticks
1 tsp cloves
25 g/1 oz orris root powder
150 ml/ ¼ pt dried pine needles

PLACE MATS

65 cm/26 in. of mattress ticking 1.35 m/54 in. wide
piece of thin wadding 32.5 cm/13 in. by
22.5 cm/9 in.
ruler
piece of dressmaking chalk

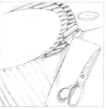

1. Mix together all the potpourri ingredients in a large bowl. Cut two pieces of ticking 32.5 cm/13 in. by 22.5 cm/9 in., then trim to an oval shape. With wrong sides together, sandwich the wadding between them. Machine together 5 mm/ ¼ in. from the edge, leaving a quarter of one edge open. Stuff with a thick layer of potpourri, spreading it out evenly. Seam up the gap.

2. Using the ruler and chalk, mark out parallel diagonal lines to make a diamond pattern. Quilt through all three thicknesses of fabric, taking care not to dislodge the potpourri.

SAGE, SORREL AND SAVORY

3. *Cut enough diagonal strips of ticking 3 cm/1½ in. wide from the remaining fabric to join up and make a bias strip at least 106 cm/42 in. long. Right sides and raw edges together, machine the bias strip around the mat, using the original stitching line as your guide. Fold over, press, then turn under and hem the remaining raw edge on the underside of the mat.*

TIP
You can also make an oval version of this mat, using pieces of ticking measuring 38 cm/15 in. by 28 cm/11 in. and drawing the oval shape freehand within the rectangle.

SAGE, SORREL AND SAVORY

HERBAL DYES

HERBS HAVE been used for dyes and colourings ever since the days when our ancestors painted themselves with woad. Sorrel has been used since medieval times to dye cloth. If you use the roots of sorrel you should get a dusky pink colouring, while the leaves and stems produce a subtle yellow. Use only natural fibres such as silk, wool, cotton or linen for dying; man-made fibres simply will not 'take'.

❖ First wash your material thoroughly. If you are using virgin wool you will need to wash it several times to remove the natural lanolin. End with a final rinse in vinegar.

❖ You will need to add something to 'fix' the colour. Alum is the mordant that is normally used with sorrel. Buy it from a pharmacy, you will need 25 g/1 oz for every 450 g/1 lb material.

❖ Use an equal weight of sorrel to the weight of the fabric i.e. 450 g/1 lb herb to 450 g/1 lb cloth.

❖ Dissolve the alum in a little hot water, put it in a dye bath or bucket, then add another 20 litres/4 gallons water. Put in the fabric to be dyed, bring very slowly to the boil and simmer for one hour – the water temperature should be about 50°C/125°F. Rinse the fabric and it is ready for dyeing.

❖ Chop the leaves of the sorrel or crush the roots with a hammer. Put it in a bag made from cheesecloth or a piece of old nylon net curtain. Leave to soak overnight in a large bucket, enamel bowl or preserving pan.

❖ Then bring the mix to the boil and simmer for up to 3 hours, or until the water has taken on the colour you want.

❖ Take out the bag of sorrel, cool the mix, then immerse the fabric and simmer for one hour.

❖ Leave the fabric to cool in the water, then take out and rinse in warm, then cold, water. Finally, hang out to dry.

TIP
If you are dyeing wool to
make a sweater, always do an extra
hank so you have yarn left for repairs.
You will never be able to duplicate
the exact shade again.

77

THYME, TANSY AND TARRAGON

PLANT CARE

THYME
Thymus

This small bushy perennial is a native of hot dry hillsides, so it needs well-drained soil and as much sun as possible. Thyme prefers some protection from the wind. Upright thymes reach up to around 30 cm/12 in. in height, while creeping thymes only rise a fraction of that above ground level.

Sow the seed in late spring where it is to grow, then thin the seedlings of most thymes out to about 30 cm/12 in. apart. Creeping thymes should be placed 20 cm/8 in. apart.

If a patch of thyme looks dead in the centre and you don't want to divide it, try heaping a spadeful of soil over it, and it should regenerate. Despite the fact that thyme can handle drought, young plants should be watered frequently until they have settled in.

> **TIP**
> All thymes should be cut back after flowering. Trim them with garden shears. If your thyme forms over-large clumps after a year or so, these should be split up, trimmed of dead wood and re-planted.

TANSY
Tanacetum vulgare

A hardy perennial, tansy grows to 90 cm/36 in. high. It will thrive almost anywhere, but does not like a waterlogged soil.

Sow tansy in the spring. The seed is almost like dust, so it is better started indoors. Sow the seed on the surface of a seed-tray, then cover with a light dusting of potting mixture.

Grown tansy plants can be divided in autumn or spring. Cut them back after they have flowered. Tansy makes a handsome foliage plant in a mixed border, particularly among tall, strong-growing perennials such as goldenrod (*Solidago*).

However, if it is left unchecked it can tend to take over and swamp other more delicate plants in the bed, so divide it frequently.

The easiest way to propagate thyme is by layering. Peg an outside branch to the ground, using a large hairpin or piece of bent wire, then heap soil over the centre of it.

Large clumps of tansy benefit from being divided into smaller plants. Split the root using a sharp spade.

TARRAGON
Artemisia dracunculus/dracunculoides

Of the two kinds of tarragon, the best, French tarragon (*A. dracunculus*) is a tender perennial plant which grows to about 90 cm/36 in. in height and is best grown in a pot that can be put somewhere frost-free in winter. The taller, coarser Russian tarragon (*A. dracunculoides*), on the other hand, is hardy in cooler climates and reaches a height of 120 cm/48 in. or more.

Both like a sheltered sunny place to grow, with a rich well-drained soil.

Sow Russian tarragon from seed, starting it off in seed-trays, then transferring the seedlings to the garden when they are large enough. French tarragon can only be started from cuttings and root cuttings are best.

TIP
Tarragon hates being overshadowed by the leaves of other, larger plants, so make sure it gets plenty of sun to itself.

ABOVE *Harvest thyme frequently to keep it green and bushy.*

Pull off a piece of root with nodules on it and raise in potting mixture.

HARVESTING

ALL HERBS should be cut before noon if possible, when the leaves are no longer wet from overnight dews but when the sun has not yet leached out the vital oils that give them their flavour.

HARVESTING THYME

You can take several cuttings a year from thyme for drying. But, unlike most herbs, thyme has its best flavour when it is flowering. Cut thyme for drying in the early morning, the moment the dew has dried, to make the most of its fragrant oils. Tie the branches into small posies using twine or thread. Keep different varieties of thyme apart from each other and their scents and flavours will be different. For culinary use, pick thyme leaves freshly as you need them. As the plant is an evergreen perennial you will have a supply all year round.

HARVESTING TANSY

Pick bunches of tansy leaves to hang around the house to discourage insects. Cut them back at the base of the stem and either make them into bunches to hang up right away or make them up into bundles for drying. If you are picking tansy flowers for potpourri, gather them when they are fully open. Keep them away from other herbs until you actually want to mix them – the smell of tansy can contaminate other plants.

LEFT *Use the tansy when it is freshly picked.*

HARVESTING TARRAGON

Tarragon leaves are at their best in late summer. Cut the branches back by no more than two-thirds, that way they will produce fresh new growth. If you are picking tarragon to use for cooking, pick the leaves just before you want to use them as they wilt very quickly.

Tarragon is one of the greatest of all culinary herbs.

THYME, TANSY AND TARRAGON

1. *Pour the tepid yeast mixture into the bread mix in the bowl and stir with a wooden spoon until it makes a dough.*

2. *Make regular indentations in the risen dough with your fingers and push the olives into them.*

82

THYME FOCACCIA

THIS TYPICALLY simple Italian country bread is traditionally cooked on a stone or under a mound of ashes in the hearth. It tastes delicious, especially made with fresh thyme and black olives.

INGREDIENTS

Makes 1 x 700 g/1½ lb loaf

425 ml/¾ pt tepid water
½ tsp sugar
1 sachet of dried yeast
700 g/1½ lb strong white flour
2 tsp salt
2 tbs finely chopped thyme
1½ tbs olive oil
125 g/4 oz black olives, pitted

TIP

If you can't get fresh herbs to add to your home-made focaccia, dried ones will do, but add only half the quantity shown in the recipe.

✤ Put the tepid water in a bowl and sprinkle with the sugar and yeast. Leave in a warm place for about 15 minutes until it starts to froth.
✤ Mix the flour, salt and half the thyme together in a large bowl, then add the oil. Make a hole in the centre and pour in the yeast mix. Stir with a wooden spoon, gradually taking in the flour from the sides until thoroughly combined. Knead into a firm dough that leaves the sides of the bowl clean.
✤ Cover the bowl with a damp tea-towel and put somewhere warm to double in size.
✤ Turn the dough out onto a greased baking sheet and punch it down, spreading it with your fingers or a flour-dusted rolling pin to make a rectangular shape.
✤ Brush the top with extra olive oil and sprinkle with the remaining thyme. Poke regular indentations in the top of the dough and push olives in them.
✤ Bake in a preheated oven at 230°C/450°F/gas mark 8 for about 35 minutes, or until the top is just turning golden brown.

TANSY MAYONNAISE

YOU CAN make the basic mayonnaise in a blender instead of by hand. Use shop-bought mayonnaise if you prefer as a short cut.

TIP
To make the classic sauce tartare, simply add a tablespoon of lemon juice and 2 teaspoons of capers to this recipe, substituting 1 teaspoon of tarragon for the tansy.

INGREDIENTS

1 egg yolk
1 tsp French mustard
½ tsp salt
¼ tsp pepper
1½ tsp sugar
juice of 1 lemon
150 ml/¼ pt oil
1 tsp finely chopped young tansy leaves
2 tsp finely chopped parsley

❖ Put the egg yolk in a bowl with the mustard, salt, pepper, ½ tsp of the sugar and 1 tsp of the lemon juice. Mix thoroughly, then beat in the oil, drop by drop, until the mixture is thick and smooth. When all the oil has been added, add 3 more teaspoons of lemon juice.

❖ Stir in the tansy, parsley and remaining sugar. Mix well, then stir in a further 2 tsp lemon juice. Serve with egg salad, or fried, grilled or barbecued fish.

❖ This mayonnaise will keep for several days in the refrigerator. Strain off the herbs after two or three days for a less pungent flavour.

TARRAGON PESTO

T HE DISTINCTIVE, almost aniseed-like flavour of tarragon makes a multitude of accompaniments to serve with meats, cheeses and eggs. Use tarragon pesto with pasta as a change from the more usual version made with basil.

INGREDIENTS

Serves 4

50 g/2 oz butter
1 tbs parsley
2 tbs tarragon leaves
2 cloves garlic
3 tbs pine nuts or walnuts
120 ml/4 fl oz olive oil
125 g/4 oz grated Parmesan cheese

❖ Soften the butter (preferably in a microwave oven).
❖ Liquidize the parsley, tarragon, nuts and garlic with the olive oil in a blender, or grind with a pestle in a mortar.

TIP

If you find the mixture
too overpowering, use the
walnuts rather than the pine nuts.
Try tarragon for flavouring a dip for
crudités and as a basis for
other sauces.

A CARTWHEEL

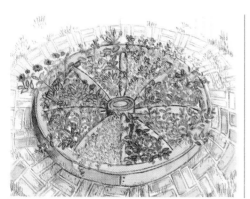

AN OLD cartwheel makes a perfect way to show off herbs. You could paint it a bright colour – turquoise for instance – and then put your plants between the spokes, alternating golden-leaved herbs like golden marjoram with those that are greenish-blue, like rue, or silvery, like 'silver posie' thyme. If you haven't got a real cartwheel to play with, you could lay out pieces of wood to make the same shape. It also looks good using small pieces of rock to form the outer circle. Another idea that works well is to make a cartwheel shape, on a larger scale, out of small bricks.

WOODEN LADDER

IF YOU have a ladder that is unusable because some of the rungs are unsafe, lay it flat in the garden and use its shape as an edging for the smaller herbs, with the rungs bordering their territory. You could cut the ladder in half, of course, and make two matching beds that way, either side of a path. If a conventional ladder is too small-scale for your garden, consider making a ladder-shaped frame for your plants out of bricks. They could either form paths between the herbs, or the structure could be raised to make a low ladder-shaped bed, forming the edge of a patio perhaps.

An old cartwheel
makes an effective display
for herbs.

THYME, TANSY AND TARRAGON

1. *Plant the prepared box with prostrate varieties of thyme. Plant upright varieties along the back and sides to make a decorative edging.*

RIGHT *A stone wall makes a useful instant seat, especially if it has something aromatic like thyme growing over it.*

A THYME SEAT

MAKE A scent-covered seat for your garden. It could overlook your herb plot or be put in a sunny corner. If you have a slope or a high bank of soil, you could simply cut a 'step' into it and plant it with thymes or allow thyme to cascade over a low-level wall. Or you can build your own, using bricks, breeze-blocks or old railroad ties for the frame.

Construct a 'box' on the ground at the site where you want the seat to be. The easiest way to make this is from breeze-blocks or some similar material, but you could construct it out of hardwood.

It should be 45 cm/18 in. high and a minimum of 30 cm/12 in. deep and 40 cm/16 in. wide – though it would be better to make it double the width as a seat for two.

Half-fill the box with pebbles or rubble for drainage, then fill it to the brim with soil, tamping it down well. Leave it for several weeks to settle down, adding more soil as the level drops. Eventually you will have a firm 'seat' with which to work.

Plant up the soil with thymes, choosing prostrate varieties. Go for perfumes such as that from the tiny *thymus azoricus* which makes a good compact 'pillow' for the seat and smells of pine needles. At the back and along the sides, however, you could put upright thymes to make a decorative edging. If you have made your seat from breeze-blocks, face them with a cement mix or disguise them by growing a row of lavender or rosemary in front.

Give your thymes at least one summer season to grow before you attempt to sit on your perfumed seat – avoid doing so, by the way, early in the morning when the dew is on it, or after rain, or you may have a wet surprise!

Thyme is not the only plant you can use for a herb seat. You could plant it with tiny creeping Corsican mint, which makes a firm, tightly-knit carpet, or use a mixture of marjorams. Turn your seat into a bower by framing it into an armchair, planting tightly-clipped rosemary on top to surround three sides of the seat.

A HERB PRESS

NCE YOU have discovered just how decorative pressed herbs can be, you'll find all sorts of uses for them around the house – try using them to decorate painted furniture, for instance. If you glue them in place, then cover them with five or six layers of varnish, your decoration will last indefinitely. If you are using herbs on any scale you'll need to have a herb press. Make your own – it is quite simple to do.

MATERIALS

2 pieces of 20 cm/8 in. square plywood
6 pieces of 20 cm/8 in. square card
4 long bolts
4 washers
4 wing-nuts

1. *Drill four holes to take the four bolts just in from the corners of both pieces of plywood, making sure that the holes line up. Diagonally trim the corners of the card.*

2. *Assemble the press by pushing the bolts through the plywood, ends upward, from the bottom to the top. Using the washers, screw the top down with the wing-nuts, screwing each one down a little in turn so that the plywood does not distort. Put your herbs between the card, placing them between two sheets of tissue, then a folded sheet of copy paper.*

3. *Screw the press down and leave for a day or so, then unscrew to see how your herbs are doing. Paint your press, then decorate with cutout pictures of herbs and flowers. Glue them to the plywood, then give them several coats of acrylic varnish.*

TIP

If you get the plant pressing bug, make yourself several presses, both small and large, using the same basic technique shown on this page.

Thymus vulgaris · Tanacetum vulgare · Artemisia dracunculus · Thymus vulgaris · Tanacetum vulgare · Artemisia dracunculus · Thymus vulgaris · Tanacetum vulgare · Artemisia dracunculus · Tanacetum vulgare ·

ACKNOWLEDGEMENTS

The publishers would like to thank
the following companies for their help:

BASKETS AND GLASSWARE
Global Village,
Sparrow Works, Bower Hinton, Martock, Somerset, UK
Telephone: +44(1935) 823390

DRIED HERBS AND FLOWERS
The Hop Shop,
Castle Farm, Shoreham, Sevenoaks, Kent TN14 7UB, UK
Telephone: +44(1959) 523219

HERB PLANTS BY MAIL ORDER
Jekka's Herb Farm,
Rose Cottage, Shellards Lane, Alveston, Bristol BS12 2SY, UK
Telephone: +44(1454) 418878

HERB SEEDS
Suffolk Seeds,
Monks Farm, Pantlings Lane, Coggeshall Road,
Kelvedon, Essex CO5 9PG, UK
Telephone: +44(1376) 572456

PICTURE CREDITS
Harry Smith Horticultural Photographic Collection
P 67
Andrew Lawson Photography
P 75, 76, 77
S & O Matthews Photography
P 39

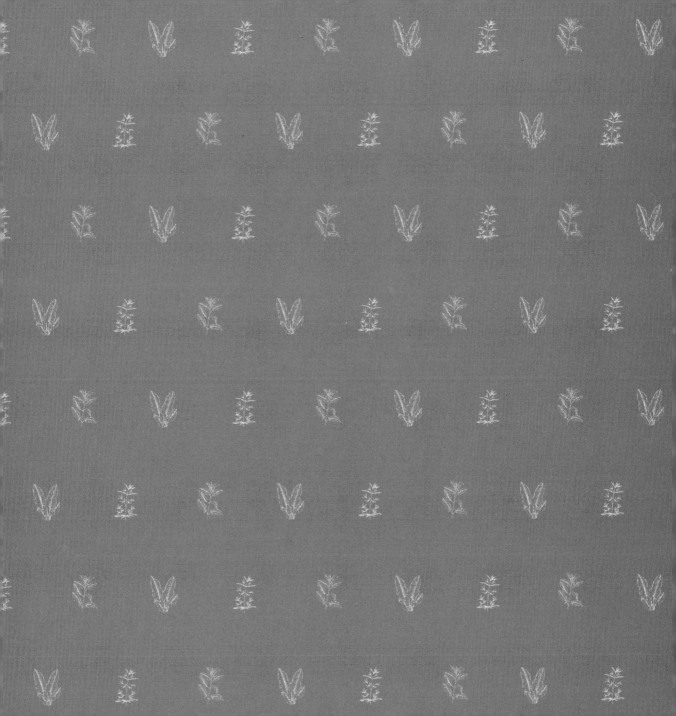

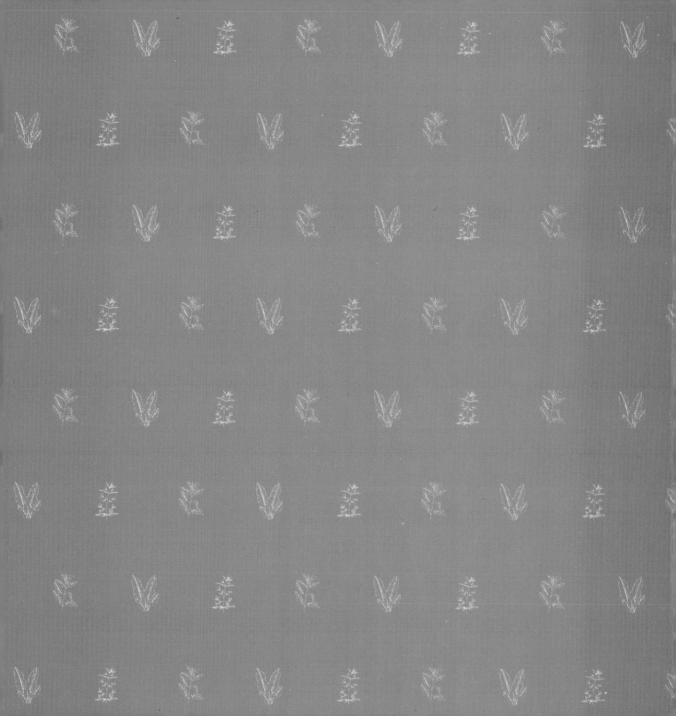